St. Therese
of the Child Jesus

REV. JUDE WINKLER, OFM Conv.

Imprimi Potest: Mark Curesky, OFM Conv., Minister Provincial of St. Anthony of Padua Province (USA)
Nihil Obstat: Francis J. McAree, S.T.D., Censor Librorum
Imprimatur: ✠ **Robert A. Brucato, D.D.**, Vicar General, Archdiocese of New York

The Nihil Obstat and Imprimatur are official declarations that a book or pamphlet is free of doctrinal or moral error. No implication is contained therein that those who have granted the Nihil Obstat and Imprimatur agree with the contents, opinions or statements expressed.

THE STORY OF A SOUL

NOT every story begins with the beginning. Our story of St. Therese actually begins toward the end of her life.

One evening Therese, who was a Carmelite sister, was telling some of the other sisters a number of stories about what had happened to her when she was young and how she had learned about God's love.

Mother Agnes, the head of her community, was so impressed by what Therese said that she asked her to write the stories down. She told Therese that these stories might be very helpful to the other sisters for they would certainly teach them about God's ways.

So in her spare time Therese began to write her account. This first book spoke especially about Therese's earliest years. When Therese finished it, she gave it to Mother Agnes.

Later, Therese's sister, Sr. Marie of the Sacred Heart, asked her to write down some more of these things. Therese wrote her sister a ten page letter, telling her all sorts of things.

THE COMPLETION OF HER WORK

FINALLY, Mother Agnes realized that Therese was very ill and that she would not live much longer. She asked her to write still another account, this time about her life as a sister. Therese once again obeyed and wrote a third account, finishing this last book with the word "love."

These three accounts tell us the story of Therese. We are very fortunate, for most of the time when we hear the stories of people's lives, we hear them told by outsiders. They try to guess what people were thinking and why they did things, but they often do not really know for sure.

Therese gave us an inside look at what she was thinking and how she loved God. This is why her stories have been called "The Story of a Soul." She did not write about herself because she wanted to be famous. She wrote her life story because she was obeying what her superior told her to do.

After Therese died, the sisters in her community realized that her story was too important to be forgotten. They published her biography, and people all over the world came to know about the life story of this gentle woman.

THE STORY OF A HOLY FAMILY

THERESE was born on January 2, 1873. Her parents, Louis and Zelie Martin, were loving parents. She had four older sisters: Marie, Pauline, Leonie, and Celine.

Therese's family was very loving, and she was cared for by both her parents and her older sisters. She was very fond of her sister Celine who was three years older than she was. Therese often shared whatever she received with Celine.

Therese was not always a quiet little girl. Her mother wrote of how little Therese had a will of her own. Once Therese said no to something, nothing could change her mind.

Therese had very beautiful memories about her mother, even though her mother died when she was only four years old.

After her mother died, Therese's father tried to be both father and mother to his girls. Therese always remembered the walks she would take with him, and how they would go to church together to pay visits to the Blessed Sacrament.

Her father also taught Therese about helping those who were poor. He would give her some money to take over to the beggars whom they would meet on their way. Therese also remembered to pray for those who were less fortunate.

A SERIOUS ILLNESS

THERESE also learned about the Catholic Faith in her everyday reading and writing lessons. The first word that she learned to read was "heaven."This must have been a great consolation to her, for she would think about her mother and pray that God had welcomed her into heaven.

Therese's sisters also taught her lessons on how to live the faith. One day when she returned home very thirsty, her sister Pauline suggested that she offer up the discomfort as a sacrifice for others.

When Therese was nine years old, her sister Pauline left home to enter the convent of the Carmelite sisters. This was a great shock for Therese, and she fell ill almost immediately.

She suffered for about three months. It was so serious that her family was afraid she might not survive.

Her family had a very strong devotion to the Blessed Virgin Mary, especially under the name of Our Lady of Victory. They prayed to her that Therese might be healed.

Our Lady answered their prayers. Therese saw the statue of Our Lady of Victory in her room smile at her, and from that moment on she began to recover.

RECEIVING THE SACRAMENTS

AFTER Pauline's departure, Therese's next oldest sister, Marie, took over the task of teaching Therese about her faith. She taught her how to pray out loud. (No one taught her how to pray in her heart, for she seems to have known how to do that on her own.)

When Therese was ten years old, she received her First Holy Communion. She later wrote about how important it was to her. She said, "What comfort it brought to me, that first kiss our Lord imprinted on my soul. I knew that I was loved, and I, in my turn, told Him that I loved Him, and was giving myself to Him for all eternity."

She was so happy that she began to cry. Some people wondered whether it might be because she missed her mother, but she said that she knew that her mother was in heaven. These were simple tears of joy.

The next June Therese received the Sacrament of Confirmation. In this sacrament she received the gift of the Holy Spirit, the spirit of God's love. She later said that it prepared her heart for all that she would have to suffer later in her life.

A GREAT CONVERSION

IT was not always easy for Therese. She was a very sensitive person, and she was often troubled by many doubts. She wondered about whether her choices were good or bad. Often simple little things disturbed her for a long time.

Then she received a special grace from the Lord. She noticed it one Christmas eve.

She had arrived home with her father after attending Midnight Mass. Her father would put her gifts inside of one of her shoes, and she would take the gifts out one by one, expressing more and more joy.

But her father was not in a good mood that night and he made a comment that this was the last year that he would have to go through that trouble.

Normally, a comment like that would have ruined everything for her, but Therese was able to deal with it. She went down and took out her presents just as she would always have done.

Therese speaks of how this opened a whole new stage of her life. She was no longer a baby. She was now ready to begin a new adventure.

CALLED TO THE CONVENT

IT was not too long after this, when Therese was fourteen and a half, that she heard the call to become a Carmelite sister. Her sister Celine was very pleased for her, but she was concerned about telling her father. Three of her sisters had already entered the convent, and she wondered whether he would allow her to go as well, especially considering how young she was.

Therese waited until Pentecost Sunday to tell her father. As he listened, his eyes filled with tears when he heard what she was proposing. He was not against it, but he did tell her that she was still too young to make such an important decision.

Nonetheless, Therese continued to explain her choice to her father and he soon gave in. She told her aunt and uncle and then brought her idea to the priest who would make the decision as to whether or not she could enter the convent.

The priest was very hesitant. One did not enter the convent at fifteen. Only those twenty-one or older were allowed to enter the convent.

But Therese had a way of changing people's minds. The priest finally told her that he was only the bishop's representative. If the bishop would agree to let Therese enter, he would not oppose it.

VISITING THE BISHOP
AND THE HOLY FATHER

AND so Therese's father took her to their local bishop. She asked him for permission to enter the convent, but he seemed to be against it. He suggested she stay with her father for a few more years to comfort him.

But Therese's father began to argue that she was right and should be allowed to enter the convent. The bishop was surprised when he heard this. He told them both that he could not make his decision until he spoke to his representative at the convent, the priest with whom Therese had already spoken. It did not look too promising.

While they were still waiting for a response, Therese, her sister Celine, and their father traveled to Rome. There they were able to meet with the Holy Father, Pope Leo XIII. She was brought before the Holy Father to receive his blessing. Therese was not supposed to say anything, but she could not hold it in.

Therese asked the Pope for his permission to enter the convent. The Pope turned to Therese's bishop who was standing at his right hand. He explained what was going on. At this point, the Holy Father told Therese to obey her superiors, but he also said, "If God wants you to enter, you will."

ENTERING THE CONVENT

THERESE returned home and waited for the bishop's answer to her request. It was New Year's Day when she finally heard that the bishop had given his approval for her to enter the convent later that year.

On the 9th of April, she finally saw the fulfillment of her desire for that was the day she entered the Carmelite convent. She was overjoyed, but she was not unrealistic about her life in the convent. It was not always easy for her, but Therese even embraced the moments of suffering with love.

Her father had grown unhealthy, and over the next couple of years his health grew worse and worse. Fortunately, he was feeling well enough to be present when his daughter was dressed in the habit of the Carmelite sisters.

He was not able to be there, though, when Therese pronounced her vows on September 8, 1890. Vows are promises that one makes to the Lord. She promised poverty (that she would own nothing of her own), chastity (that she would not marry), and obedience (that she would obey her superiors and God). Then, on September 24, she received her Carmelite veil.

Therese's father grew weaker and weaker until he died on Sunday, June 29, 1894.

A LIFE OF SIMPLICITY

THERESE had taken the name Sr. Therese of the Child Jesus when she professed her vows. This was a perfect name for her because she felt that God had called her to serve him with childlike simplicity.

She compared the Saints to flowers. Some were called to be great and beautiful lilies or roses. Others were called to be simple violets. God needed all these flowers to make his garden complete. She regarded herself as a little flower that would praise God in her everyday actions.

She prayed for others in secret, especially those who annoyed her. She offered up hidden sacrifices for sinners. Even her failures gave her joy for she recognized that these presented her with the opportunity to grow.

Therese wrote, "I was a very little soul that could offer to God only very little things. It would happen that I frequently missed the opportunity of welcoming small sacrifices that bring so much praise, but I did not then become discouraged. I bore the loss of a little peace, and I tried to be more watchful in the future." She was saying that we are not always perfect, but we can always learn from our mistakes and do it better the next time.

NOVICE MISTRESS

THERESE continued to grow in the love of the Lord. This was obvious to everyone around her.

It was for this reason that she was named the acting Novice Mistress in 1893. Novitiate is a period of special prayer and spiritual discernment. Communities choose someone as Novice Mistress who can help the young sisters to learn about the ways of the Lord. Who better to teach the young novices than Therese?

But Therese did not believe that she could do it alone. She prayed, "Lord, I am such a poor thing. I do not have it in me to give these children of yours their food. If you want each of them to get what she needs, you will have to put it here, in my hand. I will simply pass on what you give me to each soul that comes to me for its food." In saying this, she was not speaking about food for the body. She was speaking about food for the soul.

The most important lesson that she shared with the novices was her "little way." She reminded them that most of us are not called to do great things, but all of us are called to show God's love in the everyday things we do. Doing simple things well and with love is very pleasing to God.

SERVING THE MISSION

IN 1895, Therese had another important moment of conversion. She was shown a letter from a young man who was studying for the priesthood who asked whether one of the sisters might offer prayers and sacrifices on his behalf.

From then on Therese dedicated herself to the spiritual help of those around her. If she suffered, she offered up that suffering for those who were sinners and who were therefore suffering spiritually. If she prayed and yet could not feel God's love in return, she then would pray that others might feel that love even if she did not.

Therese felt that she was called to be a missionary, but God had another plan. Because of her responsibilities and her poor health, she never had the chance to go to the missions herself.

Yet, she was continuously praying for those in the missions and she offered up many sacrifices for them. (When we give up something as an expression of love, that love can be dedicated to those who need it most.) Through her prayers and offerings, she did more good for the missions than many of those who actually work there.

It was for this reason that Pope Pius XI named her the Patron Saint of the Missions, for her heart had always been there.

TOTAL SURRENDER

THUS, on June 9, 1895, Therese totally surrendered herself to God's love. She offered herself to the Lord in the place of anyone who deserved to be punished for what he or she had done. She would bear their punishment so that they could experience God's love.

Therese wrote, "My Carmelite Mother allowed me to offer myself thus to God. Flames of love, or rather oceans of grace filled my soul. Since that day love surrounded and penetrated me: at every moment God's merciful love renewed and purified me, cleansing my soul from all traces of sin."

It was less than a year later, in April of 1896, that Therese was granted what she had asked for: to suffer for those who had lost their way. She began to experience the symptoms of a terrible disease that would bring on her death a year later. That disease was tuberculosis.

Throughout the first year of her illness, Therese continued to follow the everyday activities of the convent. She did not feel sorry for herself. She did not get angry or nasty. She believed that her loving Lord had called her to this hour of suffering, and she accepted it as best she could. God had called her to the cross, and she took up that cross with all her love.

GREAT SUFFERING

THE suffering was horrible. Before Therese died, she said, "I did not think it was possible to suffer so much."

It was not easy to trust in God's love in the midst of all this suffering. When she would experience temptations to doubt God's mercy and love, she would even offer up those moments of doubt for those who had doubts about their faith.

During much of this period she was writing her book of remembrances. Eventually she was so weak that she could not even hold a pen in her hand. She would write her notes with a pencil until even that fell from her hands.

She entrusted herself to the Blessed Virgin. One day she sang, "When will it come, O tender Mother? When will that beautiful day come, that day on which from this earthly exile I shall fly to my eternal repose?"

Even when Therese was suffering so terribly, she was thinking of others. She knew that she was dying, but yet she said, "How unhappy I shall be in heaven if I cannot do little favors on earth for those whom I love."

A SAINT'S DEATH

ON September 30, 1897, our Lord called Therese home to heaven. The very last words that she spoke were, "My God, I love you."

When Therese passed away, she was all but unknown. Only a few sisters even knew that she had written an account of her life and spiritual journey. Mother Agnes, the sister who had encouraged Therese to write these things, sought to have them published. She did not receive much encouragement, but eventually the sisters had 2,000 copies printed. The sisters worried that no one would be interested in the book.

But the exact opposite happened. Only three years after the book was printed, the convent at Lisieux was receiving fifty letters a day requesting information about Therese's little way. Three years later, they were receiving five hundred letters a day.

Therese became so popular that Pope Pius XI spoke of her "hurricane of glory." Normally, there was a waiting period of fifty years after death before a person could be beatified. But Pope Pius XI beatified Therese in 1923 and canonized her only two years later, on May 17, 1925. She was the Saint of the Simple and the Everyday. She taught us that one did not have to do great things to be pleasing to the Lord.

DOCTOR OF THE CHURCH

ST. Therese's feast day is October 1. Many people pray for her intercession, and they often speak of seeing roses as a sign that their prayers will be answered.

In 1997 Pope John Paul II declared St. Therese to be a Doctor of the Church. Normally, Doctors of the Church are people who write long books or who teach great and profound things. St. Therese, in her childlike simplicity, taught a truth as profound as any other Doctors of the Church. She thought of herself as being a small violet in a garden filled with great lilies, but she was just as beautiful as they were.